This book is lovingly dedicated to my husband, Bill,
and our children, Lauren and Michael.

Acknowledgments

The best part of writing this book was meeting and talking with the wonderful collectors who share the same desire for knowledge on our hobby. I would like to thank the following collectors for allowing me to photograph some of their doorstops. Without their cooperation, this book would not have been possible. Betty Baskin, Bob Brady, Norma & Luther Conant, David Davies, Jeanette & Craig Dinner, Sybil (Cal) Gagliardi, Adriene & Ed Hoffman, Jack Nissim, Gail Skemp, Lynda & Mark Suozzi, Vita & Erik Swartz, Iris Zakarin, and especially to Frank Whitson for not only sharing his doorstops, but for his encouragement, knowledge, and friendship.

Most of all, I owe a very special thanks to my husband, Bill, for without his help, patience, and support, this book would never have been written.

Table of Contents

Introduction

Due to their newfound popularity, more and more doorstops are finding their way onto shelves, appearing at antique shows, flea markets, and auctions. New finds are constantly being made by collectors and dealers. Their desirability is increasing due to the new collectors entering this hobby of collecting.

This rapidly growing demand for doorstops has created a need for a reference book to which both collectors and dealers alike can turn. My objective in writing this book is to aid both beginners and advanced collectors by providing photos and descriptions of many different doorstops along with a value/rarity guide.

Many more doorstops exist than are shown in this book. Readers should realize that this book is merely an introduction to the hobby and is not meant to be a complete work.

In the many collections I viewed and photographed, there were some bookends and/or garden ornaments. Although I chose to photograph only doorstops (when known), I did include the garden ornaments and indicated each. I feel that although they were not produced as doorstops, they may have been used for that purpose. Even as garden ornaments, their desirability is about the same as a doorstop because of their size and because they are full figured.

I did not include bookends, on the other hand, because I feel values should be less than doorstops. When purchasing a single bookend, it is half of the original set.

Readers should realize that as more sources of information surface, some doorstops pictured may prove to be bookends and values will change.

I have included sizes for each doorstops listed which will make identification easy. If a doorstop that is not listed is in question of being a bookend, a few general guidelines can be applied. First is its size. Generally most doorstops stand 6" to 14" high. There are exceptions, though, such as 5½" doorstops of a stork, a cat, a duck, and a little black girl designed by Hubley for nursery doors or for a child's room. The wedge, designed to lodge under the door, is a key that they are doorstops.

The other guideline would be its weight. Most doorstops are heavier than bookends that were manufactured within the same years. Through the years, companies cut costs by reducing the amount of iron used. Therefore, doorstops made in the late 1930's and 1940's will generally feel lighter than the earlier ones, with bookends following suit.

When known, I have listed the manufacturer of the doorstop. Since catalogue references are scarce and incomplete, identification of manufacturers is difficult. Occasionally the piece may be marked or signed, which makes identification easy. Therefore, I have included pages of a company catalogue available to aid in identifying some doorstops.

I hope this book proves helpful to the beginner or advanced collector. Doorstop collecting can provide all the pleasures and satisfaction of most collecting hobbies: the thrills of the search; the excitement of a new and perhaps rare find; and the joys of ownership.

If you have any comments or questions or would like to join a doorstop collectors club, feel free to contact me at 2413 Madison Ave., Vineland, NJ 08360. I would also be interested in hearing of any doorstops not featured in this book for a future volume.

Rating the Doorstops and Factors that Affect Price

There are three important factors that affect the price of a doorstop: rarity, condition, and desirability.

With any collectable item, it is only natural to assume that the rarer it is, the more it is worth. Most collectors are proud to own a one-of-a-kind doorstop. As the popularity of doorstop collecting increases, more sources of information will surface with more doorstop finds being made. What is thought to be rare today may turn out to be more plentiful when other collections are brought to light.

Desirability will also affect the price of a doorstop. Some relatively common doorstops have a much higher value than some of the rarer ones. It may be a quality piece with great form or subject matter. For example, the Campbell kids, Dolly and Bobby Blake have appeared in most collections I have viewed and turn up for sale at shows frequently. Yet, because of the demand for them among collectors, their desirability merits a higher price than their rarity.

Condition is the third important determining factor of price. Mint condition, which is perfect with no blemish, is worth more than that same would bring in good condition. Good condition shows some wear and age but is still desirable with most collectors, although there will be a drop in price. Below good condition will have a drastic drop in price. And repaints, poor paint, and rust can seriously lower price.

With these three factors kept in mind and overlapping at all times, a rating system has been devised to rate each doorstop from common to rare. However, the prices in this book are meant to be only an indicator and not a Bible. Locations will affect price. Cross-collectability can have a great effect on price. For example: Aunt Jemima doorstops may appeal to an Aunt Jemima collector or Black Americana collector as well as the doorstop collector. Most of all, individual tastes vary from collector to collector. Therefore, I have compiled the opinions of several other collectors as well as myself to rate each doorstop in an unbiased way.

Reproductions and their Detection

A reproduction is a modern copy of an early piece, sometimes cast from the original pattern. They have been made by someone other than the original manufacturer. Hubley sold many of their original molds to the John Wright Company of Wrightstown, Pennsylvania, who manufactures these today. They are shown on page 173. In addition to these, I have noted with an asterisk each doorstop in the guide that I know has been reproduced.

However, as the hobby of collecting becomes more popular and values increase, more reproductions will most likely appear.

There are a few ways to tell reproductions from originals. Here are a few pointers to look for:

1. The casting. Old doorstops will usually have a smooth finish. If cast in two pieces, the seams will fit almost perfectly. Most reproductions I have seen are rough and grainy looking. If the surface looks like sandpaper and the seams are sloppy, it is likely a recent casting.
2. The finish. If the paint looks bright and freshly painted, be wary. It may be just a repaint or it could be a reproduction. However, do not confuse mint condition paint for a repaint.

The best advice is to talk with knowledgeable people. The beginner is advised to purchase only from reputable dealers or collectors who stand behind their merchandise. As your collection grows and you become more familiar with doorstops, most modern reproduction will be relatively easy to spot.

Care and Preservation of Doorstops

A very popular question asked of me is how to clean a doorstop. Probably each collector can offer a different answer. Some collectors like the look of age and prefer their doorstops with the original dust untouched.

I prefer to clean a doorstop to bring out the color and detail of the piece. After having tried many methods and techniques with much trial and error, I have found a few approaches to take. Of course the condition of the piece will dictate what cleaning method to use, if any.

If a doorstop has good original paint with just dust or dirt on it, I suggest using cotton swabs and a mild furniture spray wax which cleans, brings out color, and leaves a light wax.

Use a toothbrush with lukewarm water and a mild soap if the doorstop is quite dirty. Sometimes a mild abrasive cleaner diluted with water may be needed, though I stress extreme caution to avoid removing the original paint. Test a minor part of the piece first. Some colors, such as reds, tend to come off quite easily. After the piece is completely dry, a light coat of wax will bring out the color.

Removing a repaint is one thing I have not experimented with; it should not be attempted unless one is experienced. It is very easy to remove the original underneath paint while removing the repaint.

Chipping off the repaint with a small tool such as a file would be the safest although the most time consuming method. Nail polish remover has been mentioned to work although I would fear taking off the original also.

Whatever approach you decide to take, please use caution and take time to clean the doorstop carefully.

History

Doorstops, or doorporters as they were first called, originated in England where they were used to keep doors open to provide better room ventilation. Following the Victorian fashion imported from England, the makers of cast iron doorstops produced a menagerie of wild and domestic animals. Nearly every breed of dog was cast in great numbers. Many of these animals were full figure — cast in two parts, screwed together and painted.

Most doorstops were produced from the late 1920's to as late as the mid 1940's (with the exception of the few manufacturers who remain in business today). They were a product of the times. As their popularity increased, the variety of themes increased. They sold in gift shops at an average of about $1.50 each.

Around 1942, WWII ended production of most civilian castings and doorstops faded from the scene.

How a Doorstop is Made

All doorstops start as sand castings. Briefly, that is iron created by melting pure pig iron with scrap iron, then pouring the metal heated to about 2800°F into a sand mold. The mold contains a cavity inside that is the identical shape of the doorstop desired. The cavity is produced by a metal or wood pattern, also duplicate of the doorstop. The pattern produces the impression (cavity) by sand being compressed on it. The pattern is removed, leaving a depression in the sand the same shape as the pattern that formed it. This impression/cavity is filled with the molten iron, which cools, and the doorstop is created.

The doorstops were sprayed and hand painted. Usually a coat of one color would be sprayed over the casting, then hand painting was done in various colors to outline and highlight eyes, flowers, anything that should be prominent to create a more beautiful and detailed item.

Manufacturers

Albany Foundry Company was in existence from 1897 to 1932 on VanRensselaer Island, just south of the Albany city line. This island was incorporated in the area of the Port of Albany in 1931–1932 and the foundry closed. There seems to be no successor. The company specialized in doorstops, hitching posts, firebacks, etc. and sold these as undecorated grey iron castings. The items would be furnished decorated in color if so ordered.

UNDECORATED GREY IRON CASTINGS

Book Ends, Door Stops, Candle Sconces, Door Knockers, Candle Sticks, Andirons and Miscellaneous Castings

Made by

ALBANY FOUNDRY COMPANY

ALBANY, NEW YORK

U. S. A.

1924

Reproduction of a catalog page from the Albany Foundry Company, Albany, NY 1924

Price List, January 1st, 1924

ALBANY FOUNDRY COMPANY
ALBANY, NEW YORK

BOOK ENDS			DOOR STOPS		
No.	Per Pair	Doz. Pair	No.	Each	Doz.
2	$2.00	$22.00	1	$ .80	$ 8.80
7	.25	2.75	2	1.00	11.00
43	.85	9.25	3	.60	6.60
44	.85	9.25	4	.50	5.50
45	.85	9.25	5	.75	8.25
46	.85	9.25	6	.75	8.25
47	.85	9.25	34	1.00	11.00
48	.75	8.25	57	.75	8.25
49	.75	8.25	58	1.20	13.20
50	.75	8.25	59	.75	8.25
51	1.25	13.75	60	.75	8.25
52	1.00	11.00	72	2.00	22.00
53	1.00	11.00	75	.60	6.60
54	1.00	11.00	76	1.50	16.50
55	1.25	13.75	77	.75	8.25
56	1.00	11.00	81	1.50	16.50
75	1.20	13.20	82	1.50	16.50
78	1.25	13.75	83	1.00	11.00
79	1.25	13.75	94	1.00	11.00
80	1.25	13.75	95	1.50	16.50
83	2.00	22.00	95A	.75	8.25
84	1.00	11.00	105	.75	8.25
85	1.00	11.00	108	1.50	16.50
86	1.00	11.00	109	1.50	16.50
87	1.00	11.00	110	2.00	22.00
88	1.00	11.00	111	.60	6.60
89	1.00	11.00	113	.85	9.25
90	1.00	11.00	114	1.50	16.50
93	1.00	11.00	115	.85	9.25
116	1.25	13.75	119	1.50	16.50
117	1.25	13.75	120	1.50	16.50
			121	1.10	12.00
			123	1.75	19.25
			124	1.50	16.50

Reproduction of a catalog page from the Albany Foundry Company, Albany, NY 1924

Reproduction of a catalog page from the Albany Foundry Company, Albany, NY 1924

DESCRIPTION *of* DOOR STOPS

No.	Weight *Pounds*	Size *Inches*
1	5½	10 x 8½
34	4	9½ x 4¾
57	5	9½ x 9
58	6½	10½ x 8
59	4½	7 x 7
60	5	8½ x 7
72	8	15½ x 7
76	4½	7¾ x 4¼
81	6	12¼ x 5
82	6	12¼ x 5
95	6	6¾ x 3
95A	3¼	5 x 8
108	5½	9½ x 5
121	5½	10½ x 8
123	7½	7 x 5
124	4½	5 x 9

NOTE:—Nos. 1, 76, 95 and 121 will be drilled and tapped, at a slight expense, for receiving electric fixtures, thus converting them into lamp bases.

Nos. 95 and 95A are two separate pieces.

No. 95 may be used without the pillow (95A).

Nos. 95 and 76 are castings of the complete figure, back as well as front.

Reproduction of a catalog page from the Albany Foundry Company, Albany, NY 1924

Reproduction of a catalog page from the Albany Foundry Company, Albany, NY 1924

DESCRIPTION *of* DOOR STOPS

No	Weight *Pounds*	Size *Inches*
2	5	$7\frac{3}{4}$ x $6\frac{1}{4}$
3	$3\frac{3}{4}$	8 x $5\frac{1}{2}$
4	2	6 x 4
5	$4\frac{1}{2}$	$11\frac{1}{4}$ x 9
6	3	8 x 3
75	$3\frac{1}{4}$	$6\frac{1}{2}$ x 4
77	$5\frac{3}{4}$	$3\frac{3}{4}$ x $7\frac{1}{4}$
83	3	$7\frac{1}{2}$ x 4
94	3	10
105	5	$2\frac{1}{2}$ x 6
109	6	13 x 5
110	7	14 x 6
111	2	9 x 4
113	$4\frac{1}{4}$	8 x 7
114	$4\frac{1}{2}$	11 x 6
115	3	10 x 6
119	$4\frac{3}{4}$	13 x 7
120	6	13 x 5

Reproduction of a catalog page from the Albany Foundry Company, Albany, NY 1924

A.M. Greenblatt Studios was in operation from 1924 until 1948–1949 at 17 Richmond Street; Boston, Massachusetts, later moving to 53 Hanover Street. A. Morris Greenblatt, the owner, was first associated in 1902 with the Nubian Art Company; but later with the Boston Plastic Art Co. of which he became president/manager in 1909. Some of the doorstops signed and dated by Greenblatt Studios include Dog and Duck; Halloween Cat and Lighthouse of Gloucester, Massachusetts.

Bradley and Hubbard was started in 1854 by Walter Hubbard in partnership with his brother-in-law, Nathaniel Lyman Bradley, in Meridan, Connecticut. They manufactured cast-metal ornamental household items such as clocks, vase tables, mirror frames, andirons, sconces, lamps and chandeliers. In 1875, the firm was incorporated under the name Bradley and Hubbard Manufacturing Company. For many years the firm of B&H continued making novelty art goods such as doorstops. In 1940, the Charles Parker Company, once famous for its manufacture of the Springfield rifle, purchased the B&H Mfg. Company, by then best known for the Rayo lamp, made for the Standard Oil Company. Today referred to as the Tiffany of doorstops, many collectors feel B&H produced the best doorstops. Each is an exquisite piece, beautifully cast and detailed.

Eastern Specialty Manufacturing Company was in business from 1983 to 1930. The company had a number of addresses during this period, but was located at 64 Stanhope Street for the last few years of its existence in Boston, Massachusetts. Some of their doorstops include Owl on Books, Horse Jumping Fence, Cat, and a few houses and ships.

Hubley Manufacturing Company located in Lancaster, Pennsylvania, was founded in 1894 as a toy company making cast iron toys. In the 1920's, the company expanded their toy operation to include the Metal Art Goods line featuring bookends, ashtrays, art novelties and doorstops. They manufactured these until 1948, at which time the company sold many of the doorstop pattern molds. The company was sold to Gabriel Industries in 1955, and that company became a division of CBS in 1978. Today, Hubley is known among doorstop collectors as one of the most outstanding and important producers of doorstops. The variety of different designs was endless; hence, most collections today contain many Hubley doorstops.

Littco Products, the art line division of The Littlestown Hardware & Foundry Company, Inc., was located in Littlestown, Pennsylvania. The company, still in business today, was established in 1916, and made doorstops from about 1930 and 1942. WWII ended most of their production of civilian castings. Sales covered most of the United States, but mainly in the eastern area, and were almost totally sold to gift shops. They produced many different doorstops such as various dogs, a flower pot, sailing ship, cat, elephant, horse, and house. The most significant, though, were Aunt Jemima, Mary Quite Contrary, Huckleberry Finn, and Dutch Girl.

National Foundry, located in Whitman, Massachusetts, was founded between 1880 and 1885. The foundry made cap pistols mostly in bronze and later in cast iron. Along with andirons, candlesticks, bookends and ashtrays, doorstops became a large part of the business. They were sold as unpainted grey iron castings. Those unacquainted with best method of decorating grey iron could follow explicit directions from the catalogue. If someone had a subject in mind that was not illustrated in the catalogue, it could be added to the line by describing it fully. Since most doorstop designs were not patented, it is understandable that many of the same patterns were made by different companies. Today, called Whitman Foundry, the company produces grey iron for valves, gears, and machine tools.

Wilton Products, Inc., the oldest manufacturer of hand cast iron reproductions in the United States, is located in Wrightsville, Pennsylvania. During the peak years of doorstop production, Wilton Products manufactured various doorstop designs but are best known for their lifelike Amish Family designs. Today, Wilton Products produces more than a dozen doorstop reproductions. Among them are the flat Aunt Jemima doorstop; the Fireside Cat and Persian Cat; Cat on Base and a Bulldog.

John Wright Company, established in the 1940's, has been reproducing doorstops from the original Hubley patterns purchased when Hubley discontinued Art Line. Located in Wrightstown, Pennsylvania, they manufacture over a dozen doorstops including five flower baskets, a fruit bowl, three cats, a horse, etc. These are pictured on page 173.

Other companies that produced and usually marked their doorstops include:

Sculptured Metal Studios; Spencer, Guilford, Connecticut; Creation Company, Lancaster, Pennsylvania in business 1929 to 1930 (Crash hit and wiped company out); Virginia Metalcrafters, Waynesboro, Virginia; Vindex, Belvidere, Illinois

Other companies that only can be identified by their trademarks which appear on the backs of doorstops:

EOM Co. Toledo, Ohio

cJo   △∨△

Trade   ▽WS▽   Mark

At this point in time, companies and their history are limited. As more sources of information surface, the list of companies that manufactured doorstops will grow.

Designers

Designers often copyrighted their designs and sometimes their names may appear on the doorstops. Fish, a popular English cartoonist of the 1920's, was commissioned by Hubley to design six doorstops. They include The Tiger; Parlor Maid; Messenger Boy; Bathing Girls; Charleston Dancers; and the footmen in two sizes: Large Footmen and Small Footmen.

Fred Everett also copyrighted his work for Hubley and designed three realistic wildlife doorstops of a pheasant, quail, and geese. Each bear his signature.

Hubley also commissioned Grace G. Drayton to design a few doorstops which were very popular. They include Twin Cats; Bobby Blake; Dolly; Lil Red Riding Hood; Dolly Dimple; and Peter Rabbit.

E. Cooke is a name that appears on the back of a few doorstops although any information on him or the manufacturer is unknown at this time. His designs include Dachshund; Monkey on Barrel; Fawn; Koala; Parrot; Penguin and possibly others that are unknown at this time.

How to Use the Guide

The doorstops in this guide have been divided among four chapters and organized by subject.

Chapter 1: People Doorstops (Women, men, storybook characters)
Chapter 2: Animals (Dogs, cats, birds, horses, rabbits, etc.)
Chapter 3: Flowers and Fruit
Chapter 4: Houses, Horse Drawn Wagons, Ships, Misc.

Variations

Paint variations are not included in the book. Although most doorstops had a certain color scheme that was used, many doorstops came in more than one paint combination. Value will rarely differ because of the color.

Reading the Captions

A. Each doorstop is named. A name was assigned when not identified in a company catalogue. I apologize if I have misnamed a certain piece.

B. Measurement   Height (tallest part of doorstop to bottom)
                             Width (widest parts)

C. Definitions   *ff – full figured
                             s – solid
                             rk – rubber knobs are on the back to protect door from scratches or dents
                             **pm – pot metal

*All doorstops are assumed to be flat backed whether curved in or straight unless otherwise noted full figured.
**All doorstops are assumed to be made of cast iron unless indicated otherwise.

D. Manufacturer's name is listed whenever possible. Sometimes more than one manufacturer produced a doorstop, resulting in a different size, paint, or detailing, and the design number as it appears on the back of the piece. Any material within quotation marks appears on the doorstop itself.

E. Grading of each doorstop has been based on the item being in excellent original condition. While a few of those pictured in this book are not in this sought-after condition, all grading was made on the doorstop assuming the collector would find it in mint condition. I should also mention, this book reflects the state of the hobby as I found it in 1999.

Most common – up to $200.00
Still common – $200.00-300.00
Desirable – $300.00-600.00
Highly desirable – $600.00-1,000.00
Rare – $1,000.00 and up

The prices in this book are meant to be only a guide. The selling price will be finally determined in the marketplace by what a willing buyer will pay to a willing seller.

Prices have risen dramatically in the past five years and will continue to climb as the demand remains; therefore, expect the prices to increase 15% to 25% a year before they level out.

F. An asterisk (*) appears before the name of a doorstop when I know it has been reproduced. Read page 8 on Reproductions.

Ordinary People

*Colonial Woman, 10¼" x 5¾", Littco Products/others, (△∨△ Pat Pend), $175.00-225.00, *Southern Belle, 11¼" x 6", National Foundry/others, (72), $150.00-200.00.

Woman Holding Flowers, 8½" x 4¾", $150.00-200.00; Woman Holding Flower Baskets, 8" x 4¾", (1270), cJo, $200.00-275.00.

French Girl, 9¼" x 5½", Hubley, (23), $250.00-325.00; **Woman with Curtsy**, 9¼" x 6⅞", (12), cJo, $225.00-275.00.

Woman with Hooped Dress, 7" x 5¼", $100.00-150.00; **Woman with Flowers and Shawl**, 11" x 6¼", (42), $250.00-300.00.

Colonial Dame, 8" x 4½", Hubley, (37) $200.00-275.00; **Dutch Girl**, 6" x 3¾" ff, $150.00-225.00.

Woman holding Hat, 6⅜" x 4⅛" ff-s, $150.00-200.00; **Girl holding Bouquet**, 7⅝" x 4¾" ff, Albany Foundry Co., $175.00-250.00.

Woman holding Shawl, 8" x 3½" ff-s, $175.00-250.00; **Woman with Muff**, 9¼" x 5" ff-s, $225.00-275.00.

Woman holding Hat, 6½" x 4⅛" ff-s, $150.00-$200.00; **Girl holding Flowers**, Pot metal, 7½" x 4½" ff, $125.00-150.00.

Maid of Honor, 8¼" x 5", Hubley, $300.00-375.00; **Woman with Ruffled Skirt**, 6⅜" x 4⅞", $150.00-225.00.

Peasant Girl, 8¾" x 5", Hubley, (5), $175.00-250.00; **Woman with Hatbox**, 6¾" x 5¼", (30), $150.00-225.00.

Sitting Figure, 8" x 3¼", Hubley, $250.00-300.00; **Old Fashioned Lady**, 7¾" x 4", Hubley 296, $350.00-425.00.

Deco Nude, 9¼" x 6¼", $200.00-275.00; **Deco Girl**, 9" x 7½", (1251), cJo, $350.00-425.00.

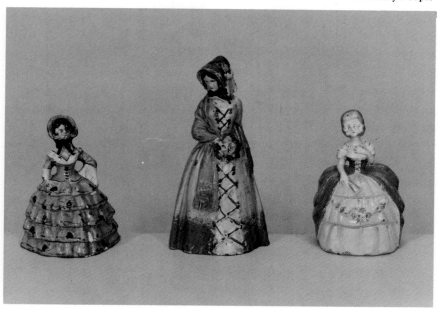

Little Colonial Lady, 4⅝" x 3⅜" ff-s, National Foundry/others, $75.00-85.00; ****Little Southern Belle**, 6¾" x 3¾" ff-s, National Foundry/others, $100.00-125.00; **Little Colonial Woman**, 4¾" x 2⅝" ff, $75.00-100.00.

Little Dutch Woman, 4" x 2⅜" ff-s, $100.00-$125.00; **Little Black Woman**, 4" x 2⅜" ff-s, $150.00-200.00; Little Colonial Woman, 4⅜" x 3¼" ff-s, $150.00-175.00.

Dancing Girl, 9½" x 6¾", National Foundry/others, (122), $400.00-475.00; **Little Girl**, 7" x 4½" ff, $250.00-325.00.

Doll on Base, 5½" x 4⅞" ff-s, $75.00-125.00; **Woman with Ruffled Dress**, 6¼" x4¾" ff, (Pat Appld For), $150.00-200.00.

West Wind, 18" x 7", English, (West Wind), $375.00-450.00; **Deco Woman**, 17" x 6½", $475.00-$550.00.

Girl Holding Dress, 13" x 6¾", (B&H 7798), $750.00-$1,000.00; **Colonial Woman**, 12⅛" x 6¼", $250.00-325.00.

Hoop Skirt Flapper, 9¼" x 6¼", (The Hoop Skirt Flapper), $550.00-600.00; **Old Woman**, 11" x7", (B&H 7796), $600.00-1,000.00.

Minuet Girl, 8½" x 5", (1278), cJo, $225.00-275.00; **Silhouette Girl**, 11¼" x 10¼", Albany Foundry, (5), $600.00-850.00.

Dutch Girl, 7⅛" x 5¾", (1255), cJo, $275.00-350.00; *__Olive Picker__, 7¾" x 8¾", (207), $650.00-$750.00.

*__Dutch Girl__, 13" x 10", (Littco Products #33, label), $375.00-450.00; **Dutch Girl with Big Shoes**, 9¾" x 9¼", $325.00-400.00.

Dutch Girl, 9¼" x 5½", Hubley, (10); $250.00-300.00, **Senorita**, 11¼" x 7", $350.00-500.00.

Maid, 8⅞" x 4⅞", (1242), cJo, $275.00-350.00; **Maiden**, 8⅞" x 3¾", $350.00-425.00.

Spanish Girl, 9⅞" x 5½", $325.00-400.00; **Woman with Fan**, 9½" x 5¼", (43), $200.00-275.00.

Spanish Girl, 9" x 5", Hubley, (192), $200.00-275.00; **Spanish Girl**, 9½" x 5¼", (Pat appld for Trade ▽ Mark), $275.00-375.00.

Queen of Scots, 6" x 5¼" ff, English, (This stone came from house of Parliament), $225.00-275.00, **Oriental Girl**, 7½" x 3¾" ff-s, $250.00-325.00.

Wine Man, 9½" x 7", $650.00–$850.00; **Geisha Girl**, 10¼" x 3½" ff, Hubley, $500.00-750.00.

Geisha, 7" x 6" ff, Hubley, $200.00-275.00; *__Small Mammy__, 8½" x 4½" ff, Hubley, **Aunt Jemima**, $200.00-300.00.

*__Aunt Jemima__, 13¼" x 8", $425.00-600.00; *__Large Mammy__, 12" x 6" ff, (Hubley Copyrighted), **Aunt Jemima**, $400.00-550.00.

Medium Mammy, 10" x 5" ff, 1 piece mold, $325.00-375.00; **Aunt Jemima**, 10½" x 6½", $350.00-400.00.

Topsy, 6" x 4" wedged, Hubley, $275.00-300.00; **Aunt Jemima**, 7½" x 3¾" wedged, $275.00-350.00.

Rhumba Dancer, 11⅛" x 6⅝", $600.00-850.00; **Tropical Woman**, 12" x 6¼", $225.00-275.00.

Jill, 8¾" x 5¾", Hubley (226), $400.00-550.00; **Girl with Bonnet**, 8" x 5¼", (Pat appld for Trade Ⓦ Mark), $475.00-600.00.

*Halloween Girl, 13¾" x 9¾", $1,000.00 and up.

Mary Quite Contrary, 15" x 8", (1292), $500.00-750.00.

*__Mary Quite Contrary__, 11⅜" x 9⅝", Littco Products, $750.00-1,000.00; *__Huckleberry Finn__, 12½" x 9½", Littco Products, $550.00-650.00.

__Lg. Sunbonnet Girl__, 9" x 5½", $400.00-450.00; __Lg. Sunbonnet Girl__, 9⅞" x 5½", $400.00-475.00.

Pied Piper, 7¼" x 5", (120), $325.00-350.00; **Little Miss Muffet**, 7¾" x 5", (121), $325.00-350.00.

Little Girl by Wall, 5¼" x 3¼" ff-s, Albany Foundry, $175.00-250.00; **Little Boy with Bear**, 5¼" x 3½" ff-s, Albany Foundry, $275.00-350.00.

***Bobby Blake**, 9½" x 5¼", Hubley, (46) $425.00-550.00; **Dolly**, 9½" x 5½", Hubley, (45), $425.00-550.00.

Lil Red Riding Hood, 9½" x 5", Hubley, (95), $425.00-550.00; ***Dolly Dimple**, 7¾" x 3¾" ff, Hubley, $325.00-450.00.

*Lil Red Riding Hood and Wolf**, 7¼" x 5⅜", National Foundry, (94), $375.00-450.00; **Lil Bo Peep**, 6¾" x 5", $225.00-300.00.

Little Red Riding Hood and Wolf, 7½" x 9½", (NUYDEA Little Red Riding Hood), $650.00-800.00; **Clown**, 8" x 3½" rk, (cJo), $550.00-650.00.

Boy with Fruit Basket, 9¼" x 3⅞", $375.00-450.00; *****Rabbit with Top Hat**, 9⅞" x 4¾", Albany Foundry, (94), $425.00-550.00.

Rabbit eating Carrot, 8⅛" x 4⅞", $400.00-475.00; **Peter Rabbit**, 9½" x 4¾", Hubley, (96), $375.00-350.00.

Grandpa Rabbit, 8⅝" x 4⅞", $1,000.00 and up; **March Hare**, 8¼" x 3¾", $425.00-500.00.

Mad Hatter, 6⅝" x 2⅞" ff, (666), $275.00-350.00; **Carpenter**, 5½" x 2¾" ff, (665), $175.00-275.00.

Girl with Beanie, 8¾" x 3¼" ff, (663), $400.00-475.00; **Humpty Dumpty**, 4½" x 3½" ff, (661), $300.00-375.00.

Popeye, 9" x 4½" ff, Hubley, (©1929 King Features Syn Made in USA), $1,000.00 and up; *__Donald Duck__, 8⅜" x 5¼", (©Walt Disney Productions 1971), $250.00-325.00.

Pinocchio, 9½" x 2¾" ff-s, lead; $650.00-800.00; **Dutch Boy**, 11" x 3½" ff, $450.00-650.00.

Colonial Pilgrim, 8¾" x 5⅜", $350.00-425.00; **Police Boy**, 10⅝" x 7¼", $550.00-750.00.

Pan and Nymph, 9¼" x 14", $850.00-1,000.00.

Reading Girls, 5" x 8⅝", $750.00-1,000.00; **Crossed Out**, 7¼" x 5⅝", (Crossed Out), $650.00-$850.00.

*Clown, 10" x 4½", $1,000.00 and up; *Organ Grinder, 9⅞" x 5¾", $375.00-450.00.

Clown, 11½" x 5½", $850.00-1,000.00; Butler, 12½" x 6", $400.00-475.00.

Sailor, 8½" x 3⅝", $250.00-325.00; **El Capitan**, 7¾" x 5¼", $175.00-250.00.

Bellhop, 8⅞" x 4⅝", (1244), $275.00-350.00; **Soldier**, 9½" x 5", Albany Foundry, $200.00-275.00.

*__Warrior__, 13¼" x 7¼", (B&H 7795), $550.00-750.00; __Knight__, 13¼" x 6", (Pat Pend), $250.00-300.00.

__Safety First Policeman__, 9½" x 5⅝", (Safety First), $650.00-800.00; __Policeman__, 7⅞" x 4", (Le Mur Lgt Co. PAT), $275.00-350.00.

Scottish Highlander, 15½" x 13", $275.00-325.00; **Vase**, 11⅞" x 8 ff, $175.00-225.00.

Man with Flowers, 9" x 5¾", $375.00-450.00; **Amish Man**, 8½" x 3¾" ff-s, $225.00-275.00.

Columbia, 16½" x 4½" ff-s, $1,000.00 and up.

Angel, 16½" x 7½", English, (8), $325.00-375.00.

George Washington, 15" x 6½" ff, $475.00-550.00; **Gaucho**, 18½" x 7 ff, $450.00-525.00.

George Washington, 12¼" x 6⅜", $425.00-500.00; **Man with Cane**, 10" x 4⅞", $400.00-450.00.

Uncle Sam, 12" x 5½", $1,000.00 and up.

Toby, 16" x 8⅜" ff, (T. Kennedy), $600.00-750.00.

Spanish Guitarist, 11" x 3⅜" ff, (△∨△Pat Pend), $600.00-750.00; **Butler**, 11¼" x 5⅞", (B&H), $650.00-800.00.

Lafayette, 11⅝" x 6⅜", $450.00-525.00; **Butler**, 10⅛" x 3¼", $425.00-475.00.

Little Heiskell Soldier, 10¾" x 6", (Little Heiskell 1769, Hagerstown, MD), $325.00-400.00; **Man with Top Hat**, 8" x 4½", (217 © J. Held Jr.), $425.00-500.00.

The Tiger, 9⅜" x 4¼", Hubley, (269 © FISH), $1,000.00 and up; **Sailor**, 11⅜" x 5", $450.00-550.00.

Parlor Maid, 9¼" x 3½", Hubley, (268 ©FISH), $1,000.00 and up; **Messenger Boy**, 10" x 5⅜", Hubley (249 © FISH), $500.00-750.00.

Bathing Girls, 10⅞" x 5¼", Hubley, (250 © FISH), $1,000.00 and up; **Charleston Dancers**, 8⅞" x 5⅜", Hubley, (270 © FISH), $1,000.00 and up.

Lg. Footmen, 12⅛" x 8¼", Hubley, (248 © FISH), $1,000.00 and up; **Guitar Player**, 11⅞" x 7⅛", (951), $475.00-575.00.

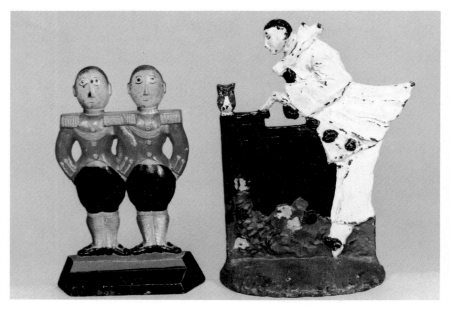

Sm. Footmen, 9⅛" x 6", Hubley, (272 © FISH), $600.00-750.00; **Harlequin**, 10⅝" x 7⅝", (© Mayfair Inc.), $1,000.00 and up.

Whimsical Man, 7" x 3½", wood wedge, (1258), $300.00-375.00; **White Caddie**, 8" x 6", $1,000.00 and up.

Buster Brown, 7¾" x 5¼", $425.00-475.00; ***Black Caddie**, 8" x 6¼", $1,000.00 and up.

*Overhead Swinging Golfer**, 10" x 7", Hubley (238), $500.00-700.00; *Putting Golfer**, 8⅜" x 7", Hubley, (34), $375.00-500.00.

Sm. Golfer, 6" x 3½" ff, $450.00-600.00; **Boy in Tuxedo**, 7¼" x 4⅜" wood wedge, $375.00-500.00.

Skier, 12½" x 5" ff, $500.00-750.00; **Drum Major**, 13½" x 6½" ff-s, $350.00-425.00.

Oriental Man, 9" x 7¼" ff, $225.00-275.00; **Buddha**, 7" x 5¾" ff, $200.00-275.00.

The Snooper, 13¼" x 4½", (The Snooper), $750.00-1,000.00; **Jungle Boy**, 12¾" x 12", $1,000.00 and up.

Rebecca at the Well, 10" x 14⅜", English, $250.00-325.00; **Boy with Hands in Pockets**, 10½" x 3⅝" ff, $350.00-425.00.

Whistling Boy, 10" x 5½" ff, rk, (429B), $400.00-475.00; **Dutch Boy**, 8⅜" x 3⅜" ff, $275.00-350.00.

Sax Player, 6⅞" x 6", $500.00-650.00; **Bellhop**, 7½" x 5⅛", $450.00-550.00.

Black Boy on Basket, 7¼" x 5" ff, Pot metal figure on iron base, $1,000.00 and up; **Major Domo**, 8⅜" x 5⅛", (1249), $175.00-250.00.

Black Man on Cotton Bale, 6⅞" x 6⅞", $1,000.00 and up; *****Cherubs**, 10" x 6⅜", $375.00-450.00.

Man in Chair, 10⅛" x 6", English, $250.00-325.00; **Man in Chair**, 9½" x 5¾", English, $250.00-325.00.

*****Ally Sloper**, 11⅛" x 6¼", English, $400.00-475.00; *****Mrs. Sloper**, 10¾" x 6⅜", English, $400.00-475.00.

65

***Punch**, 12" x 9", English, $475.00-575.00; ***Judy**, 11½" x 8¾" , English, $475.00-575.00.

Judy, 12" x 7½", English, $375.00-450.00; **Punch**, 12" x 7¾", English, $375.00-450.00.

Child Reaching, 17" x 7", (Elba Road Studroz Whitman Mass (label)), $1,000.00 and up; **Gnome with Barrel**, 14½" x 6¼" ff, $475.00-600.00.

Man with Top Hat, 9⅜" x 3⅝" ff, $275.00-325.00; **Gnome**, 10" x 4" ff, $250.00-300.00.

*Gnome, 11" x 5" ff, $225.00-275.00; **Yawning Child**, 9" x 5" ff, $200.00-275.00.

Gnome with Shovel, 9½" x 4½", $275.00-350.00; **Gnome with Keys**, 10" x 5⅜", $275.00-350.00.

Pirate Girl, 13⅞" x 7¼", (Pirate Girl), $250.00-300.00; **Pirate with Sack**, 11⅞" x9⅝", $500.00-650.00.

Pirate with Chest, 9¾" x 6", $225.00-300.00; **Pirate with Sword**, 12" x 5¾", $475.00-550.00.

Colonial Lawyer, 9⅝" x 5¼", (Trade ▽ Mark), $400.00-525.00; **The Patrol**, 8¾" x 3¾" ff, (The Patrol), $225.00-300.00.

Fisherman in Boat, 6¾" x 4", $150.00-225.00; **Old Salt**, 11" x 4⅛" ff, $225.00-275.00.

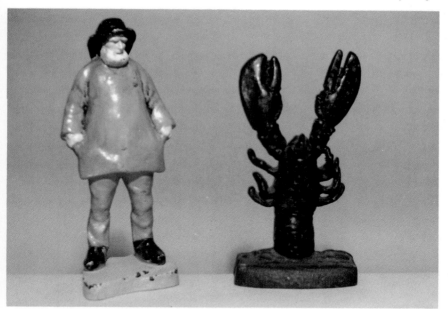

Lg. Old Salt, 14½" x 6½", $325.00-375.00; **Lobster**, 12½" x 6½", $375.00-450.00.

Cat, 7" x 4½", (Eastern Specialty Mfg. Co. #62), $350.00-425.00; **Witch**, 7" x 7", $350.00-425.00.

Animal Kingdom

Boston Terrier, 10" x 10" ff, Hubley, National Foundry/others, $75.00-125.00; **Boston Terrier with Paw Up**, 9½" x 7" ff, $375.00-450.00.

Sm. Boston Terrier, 9⅞" x 8¼", $65.00-$125.00; **Sm. Boston Terrier**, 8¼" x 8" ff, $65.00-125.00.

***English Bulldog**, 5⅞" x 8½" ff, Hubley/others, $150.00-225.00; **French Bulldog**, 7⅝" x 6¾" ff, Hubley, National Foundry/others, $125.00-175.00.

Bulldog Porcelainized, 5¾" x 8½" ff, $75.00-125.00; **Boston Terrier Porcelainized**, 8¾" x 8" ff, $75.00-125.00.

Fox Terrier, 10⅜" x 10½", $250.00-300.00; **Boston Terrier**, 9⅝" x 11¾", $350.00-450.00.

Begging Boston Terrier, 8¾" x 5" ff, $300.00-375.00; **Boxer**, 8½" x 9" ff, Hubley, $400.00-475.00.

Pug, 7¾" x 6½" ff, $175.00-250.00; **Boston Terrier Pup**, 7¾" x 8½", wedge, $150.00-200.00.

****St. Bernard**, 3½" x 10½" ff, Hubley, $375.00-500.00; **Gutter Pup**, 8½" x 7" ff, Hubley, $300.00-425.00.

*German Shepherd, 9¼" x 10" ff, Hubley, $85.00-$150.00; **German Shepherd**, 9¾" x 13" ff, Hubley, $125.00-175.00.

English Bulldog, 9½" x 5½", (B&H), $375.00-450.00; **Cairn Terrier**, 9" x 6", (B&H), $250.00-325.00.

*Double Scottie, 6¼" x 8¾", $65.00-125.00; Scottie, 8" x 8¼" ff, $150.00-225.00.

Welsh Corgi, 8¼" x 5⅞", (B&H), $200.00-275.00; *Lg. Scottie, 12" x 16" ff, Hubley, $350.00-425.00.

Boston Bulldog, 13" x 5½", glass eyes, (Greenblatt Studios), $225.00-300.00; **Dachshund**, 11⅛" x 4⅜", $400.00-550.00.

Beagle Pup, 8" x 7½" ff, $400.00-550.00; **Bronze Dog**, 9¼" x 6", $175.00-225.00.

Dachshund, 8" x 12" ff, $400.00-550.00; **Basset Hound**, 7" x 6½" ff-s, Hubley, $350.00-450.00.

Bloodhound, 6¾" x 4¼" ff, $200.00-275.00; **English Bulldog**, 5" x 4" ff, $175.00-250.00.

Beagle, 8" x 6½", $200.00-275.00; **Pekingese**, 14½" x 9" ff, Hubley, $1,000.00 and up.

Terrier Pup, 8¼" x 7½" ff, $275.00-350.00; **Spaniel**, 9" x 7", $375.00-500.00.

Yawning Dog, 7" x 5" ff, $325.00-400.00; **Sealyham**, 14" x 9" ff, Hubley, $450.00-600.00.

Japanese Spaniel, 9" x 4½", (1267), cJo, $300.00-375.00; **Malamute**, 7¾" x 6¼", $200.00-275.00.

Terrier, 4" x 7" wedge, (Spencer, Guilford, Conn.), $200.00-250.00; **Wolfhound**, 6½" x 3½" wedge, (Spencer, Guilford, Conn.), $200.00-275.00.

Terrier, 5¼" x 6" wedge, (Spencer, Guilford, Conn.), $150.00-225.00; **Lg. Fox Terrier**, 9½" x 11" ff, Hubley, $250.00-350.00.

Cocker Spaniel, 6¾" x 11" ff, Hubley, $275.00-350.00; **Springer Spaniel**, 6¾" x 7", $150.00-225.00.

Cocker Spaniel, 9" x 7" wedge, (Va Metalcrafters, Waynesboro, Va. WK, "Dream Boy 18-7 1949"), $100.00-150.00; **Bloodhound**, 15¼" x ⅜" wedge, $175.00-250.00.

Dog with Bow, 6¾" x 6½" wedge, $225.00-300.00; **Terrier with Bushes**, 8" x 7", (copt c 1929 PAL), $175.00-250.00.

Whippet, 6¾" x 7½" , $150.00-225.00; **Terrier**, 7½" x 5⅛", (#159 Copyright 1930 Creation Co.), $125.00-200.00.

Sm. Dog, 5" x 5" ff, $125.00-175.00; **Boston Bulldog**, 4½" x 4½" ff, $125.00-175.00.

Chow Chow, 8½" x 9" ff, $300.00-450.00; **Lg. Russian Wolfhound**, 9" x 16" ff, $175.00-250.00.

Pup Porcelainized, 6" x 6" ff, $125.00-175.00; ***Setter**, 8¾" x 15⅞" ff, Hubley, $175.00-275.00.

St. Bernard, 8" x 10½", $175.00-225.00; **Bird Dog**, 6" x 11¾", National Foundry, $175.00-250.00.

Doberman Pinscher, 8" x 8½" ff, Hubley, $400.00-550.00; **Whippet**, 8½" x 9" ff, $350.00-450.00.

*Puppies in Basket, 7" x 7⅜", (Copyright 1932 M. Rosenstein, Lancaster, Pa. USA), $350.00-475.00; **Mutt and his Bone**, 8¼" x 5½", (Mutt and his Bone), $175.00-200.00.

*Hunchback Cat**, 10⅝" x 7½" ff, Hubley/others, $125.00-175.00; **Beagle**, 8½" x 9⅛", $175.00-250.00.

Dachschund, 5½" x 7¼", (Taylor Cook No. 8 1930), $425.00-550.00; **Monkey on Barrel**, 8⅜" x 4⅞", (Taylor Cook No. 3 1930), $400.00-475.00.

Monkey, 7" x 5" ff, $175.00-250.00; **Cat**, 13" x 9", (Sculptured Metal Studios 1928), $275.00-350.00.

*Monkey, 8½" x 4⅝" ff, $250.00-325.00; **Cat**, 9" x 6¾", $275.00-350.00.

Cat, 10¾" x 7½", (Sculptured Metal Studios), $475.00-550.00; **Monkey**, 13½" x 5⅝", $350.00-425.00.

Cat, 11" x 7", $350.00-425.00; *****Cat**, 12½" x 7½", $175.00-250.00.

Cat, 11" x 7" ff, $150.00-200.00; ***Cat**, 14½" x 7½", $200.00-250.00.

Cat, 6¾" x 3½" ff, $85.00-150.00; **Cat**, 9¾" x 4⅜", glass eyes, $125.00-200.00.

Sleeping Cat, 7½" x 8" ff, Hubley, $450.00-550.00; ***Persian Cat**, 8½" x 6½" ff, Hubley, $175.00-225.00.

***Fireside Cat**, 5⅝" x 10¾" ff, Hubley, Littco, others, $175.00-225.00; **Sleeping Cat**, 3⅜" x 9⅝" ff, National Foundry, $275.00-350.00.

Reclining Kitten, 8⅛" x 4" ff, National Foundry, $225.00-275.00; **Cat**, 8⅜" x 5⅝", $150.00-200.00.

Sleeping Cat, 4½" x 13" ff, $750.00-1,000.00.

*Cat with Ball, 9" x 8½", $400.00-475.00; **Cat**, 10" x 3⅜" ff, Hubley, $150.00-200.00.

Modernistic Cat, 9¾" x 5 ff, Hubley, $425.00-500.00; **Cat**, 8" x 6¾", $150.00-225.00.

Halloween Cat, 9¼" x 6", (AM Greenblatt Studio #19 Copyright 1927), $300.00-425.00; **Crazy Cat**, 7" x 3¾" ff-s, National Foundry, $175.00-275.00.

Cat, 9" x 6½" ff, $150.00-200.00; **Cat**, 11½" x 7" ff, $350.00-450.00.

Twin Cats, 7" x 5¼", Hubley, National Foundry, (73) or (57), $325.00-400.00; **Crying Pup**, 7½" x 3", (662), $325.00-400.00.

*Basket of Kittens, 10" x 7", (M Rosenstein, Copyright 1932, Lancaster, PA USA), $400.00-475.00; **Crazy Cat**, 9" x 3¼" ff, $300.00-375.00.

Duck with Top Hat, 7½" x 4¼", $275.00-325.00; **Puss in Boots**, 8¼" x 5¾", $400.00-475.00.

Cat by Flower, 5" x 6¼", $100.00-150.00; **Swan**, 5¾" x 4½" ff-s, National Foundry, $200.00-275.00.

*Duck, 4" x 12¾" ff, $325.00-400.00; *Kitten, 8" x 6", Hubley, National, (38) or (37), $100.00-175.00.

Swallows, 8½" x 7½", Hubley, (480), $350.00-425.00; Quail, 7¼" x 6¼", Hubley, (459 c. Fred Everett), $350.00-425.00.

Duck, 11" x 6½", $400.00-475.00; ***Ducks**, 8¼" x 6¼", Hubley, (291), $325.00-400.00.

*Pheasant, 8½" x 7½", Hubley, (458 c. Fred Everett), $350.00-425.00; ***Geese**, 8" x 8", Hubley, (457 c. Fred Everett), $375.00-450.00.

Parrot, 8" x 3⅞" rk cJo, (1289), $175.00-250.00; **Fruits and Birds**, 6½" x 5½", (Fruits and Birds, copr 1929), $175.00-225.00.

Peacock, 6¼" x 6¼", $150.00-225.00; **Peacock**, 5⅝" x 8¼", $150.00-225.00.

Pelican on Dock, 8" x 7¼", Albany Foundry, (113), $250.00-325.00; **Heron**, 7½" x 5⅛", Albany Foundry, (83), $125.00-200.00.

Shore Bird, 10" x 6½", $275.00-350.00; **Ostrich**, 8½" x 9", (120), $225.00-300.00.

Peacock on Fence, 13" x 7⅜", National Foundry, (56), $250.00-300.00; **Bird of Paradise**, 13⅜" x 7", (LA-CS 765), $375.00-500.00.

Peacock by Urn, 7½" x 4¼", Hubley, (208), $200.00-275.00; **Camel**, 7" x 9" ff, $275.00-350.00.

Parrot in Ring, 8" x 7", rk, $125.00-200.00; **Parrot in Ring**, 13¾" x 7¼", (B&H), $225.00-275.00.

Parrot in Medallion, 9¼" x 5", $100.00-175.00; **Polly**, 8⅛" x 5¼", Hubley, (180), $125.00-200.00.

Parrot, 12½" x 7½", Albany Foundry, $125.00-200.00; **White Cockatoo**, 11¾" x 5¼", Albany Foundry, National Foundry, (82), $150.00-225.00.

White Cockatoo, 11¼" x 9½", $350.00-425.00; **Parrot**, 12½" x 6½", (Blodgett Studio, Lake Geneva, WIS #1010), $250.00-325.00.

Parrot, 7¾" x 5" ff-s, $85.00-150.00; **Parrot**, 7" x 3½", $100.00-175.00.

Chick, 5" x 5½" ff, wedge, $150.00-225.00; **Mallard**, 6¼" x 7½" ff, $275.00-350.00.

Parrot, 10⅜" x 6¾", glass eye, National Foundry, $150.00-200.00; **Squirrel**, 9" x 6⅜", $150.00-225.00.

Parrot, 8¼" x 7½", $375.00-450.00; **Owl**, 10" x 6", $225.00-300.00.

Squirrel, 8" x 5½", (EMIG 1382), $175.00-250.00; *****Squirrel**, 11" x 9½", $275.00-400.00.

Squirrel, 6" x 6", $150.00-225.00; **Squirrel Garden Ornament**, 8½" x 7" ff, Hubley, $325.00-400.00.

Owl, 9" x 5½", $275.00-350.00; **Owl**, 10" x 4½", Hubley, (254), $225.00-300.00.

Hummingbird, 4" x 7" ff, $250.00-325.00; **Owl**, 6½" x 4", $125.00-175.00.

Owl, 8¼" x 4", rk, (B&H), $300.00-375.00; **Stork**, 5½" x 3½", wedge, Hubley, $225.00-300.00.

Owl, 15½" x 5", (B&H 7797), $1,000.00 and up.

Owls on Books, 9¼" x 6½", (Eastern Specialty Mfg. Co.), $550.00-750.00; **Dog and Duck**, 10" x 8¾", (Copyright 1925 By AM Greenblatt, Boston, Mass), $750.00-1,000.00.

Duck, 9½" x 6½", $250.00-325.00; **Fawn**, 10" x 6", (No. 6 © 1930 Taylor Cook), $250.00-375.00.

Rabbit by Fence, 6⅞" x 8⅛", Albany Foundry, $375.00-450.00; **Duck by Bush**, 7½" x 10½", $375.00-450.00.

Koala, 7¼" x 5½", (No. 5 © 1930 Taylor Cook), $450.00-550.00; **Game Cock**, 7" x 5⅜" ff, $275.00-350.00.

*Rooster, 13" x 8½" , $325.00-400.00; **Turkey**, 13" x 11", $750.00-1,000.00.

Rooster, 10" x 6", $275.00-350.00; **Rooster**, 7" x 5½", $125.00-200.00.

Cockatoo, 14" x 4½" ff, $200.00-275.00; **Rooster**, 13¼" x 11", (Spencer), $600.00-800.00.

Rooster, 12" x 4½" ff, $300.00-375.00; **Duck**, 11¼" x 7" ff, $175.00-250.00.

Rabbit, 11½" x 8¾" wedge, $500.00-750.00; **Rooster**, 13" x 9", reproduction.

Rooster, 15⅜" x 6⅛" ff, $325.00-375.00; **Rabbit**, 10⅞" x 6¾", $225.00-275.00.

Rabbit Garden Ornament, 14¼" x 4⅞" ff, Hubley, $375.00-450.00; **Rabbit**, 15⅜" x 8⅜", (B&H), $750.00-1,000.00.

*Rabbit Garden Ornament, 11⅝" x 10" ff, Hubley, National Foundry, $250.00-325.00; **Wirehaired Fox Terrier**; 10½" x 12¾", Hubley, (467), $500.00-600.00.

Horse on Base, 10½" x 12¼", $125.00-200.00; **Horse on Base**, 7¼" x 8½", $150.00-225.00.

Horse Jumping Fence, 7⅞" x 11¾", (Eastern Specialty Co. #79), $400.00-475.00; **Horse**, 8" x 10", National Foundry, (12), $150.00-200.00.

Show Horse, 8½" x 8" ff, Hubley, $150.00-200.00; **Percheron**, 9" x 7¾" ff, Hubley, $175.00-225.00.

Horse, 7½" x 11" ff, Hubley, $125.00-175.00; **Horse**, 10" x 12" ff, Hubley, $125.00-175.00.

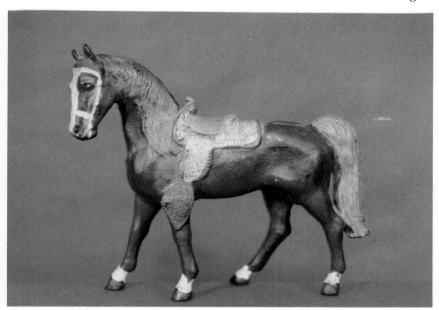

Saddled Horse, 10" x 11½" ff, $175.00-275.00.

Terrier, rubber, 12¾" x 11", (Holest Rubber Products Co., Hartford, Conn., label), $175.00-225.00; **Grazing Horse**, 8⅝" x 10½", $150.00-200.00.

Duck Head, 8" x 5¼", $100.00-175.00; **Brass Duck Head**, 11½" x 9", $100.00-175.00.

Bird by Urn, 11" x 8¼", English, $100.00-150.00; **Bird of Prey**, 16¾" x 10½", English, $125.00-200.00.

Stork, 12¼" x 7", Hubley, $350.00-450.00; **Giraffe**, 12½" x 9", Hubley, $1,000.00 and up.

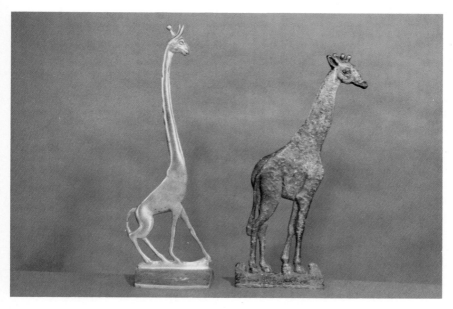

Brass Giraffe, 15½" x 4¾", wedge, $150.00-200.00; **Giraffe**, 13½" x 5¼", wedge, (S-110), $250.00-300.00.

Elk, 11" x 10", $175.00-250.00; **Elk**, 15¾" x 7", $175.00-250.00.

Lamb, 6¾" x 9¼" ff, $275.00-350.00; **Lion**, 7" x 8" ff, $125.00-200.00.

Penguin with Top Hat, 10½" x 3¾" ff, Hubley, $350.00-475.00; **Penguin**, 10½" x 5" ff, $350.00-475.00.

Parrot, 10½" x 4⅞", (No 4 c 1930 Taylor Cook), $425.00-575.00; **Penguin**, 9½" x 5¼", (No 1 c 1930 Taylor Cook), $750.00-1,000.00.

Twin Penguins, 7¼" x 7½", $175.00-250.00; **Fantail Fish**, 9¾" x 5⅞", Hubley, (464), $175.00-250.00.

*Swan, 15¾" x 6¾", $275.00-350.00.

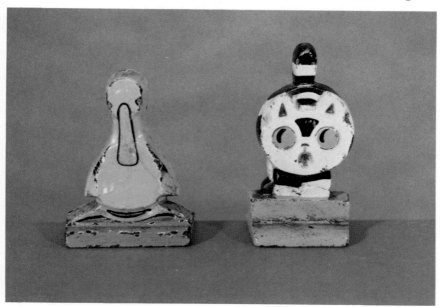

Duck, 5" x 3¾", wedge, Hubley, $250.00-300.00; **Cat**, 6" x 3", wedge, $400.00-550.00.

Woodpecker, 8½" x 6¼", $750.00-1,000.00; **Dunce Bear**, 9⅝" x 3¾", $550.00-650.00.

Woodsman, 13¼" x 9", English, $225.00-300.00; **Stork**, 13¾" x 8⅞", $350.00-425.00.

*****Cow**, 12½" x 8½", (New Holland Machine Co., Compliments of A.M. Zimmerman), $350.00-425.00; **Sheep**, 9⅝" x 7¼", $300.00-375.00.

Elephant, 5" x 8", $100.00-175.00; **Blowfish**, 8" x 7¼" ff, Hubley, $450.00-575.00.

Elephant, 8¼" x 12", Hubley, $100.00-175.00; **Elephant**, 10" x 11¾", (B&H), $250.00-350.00.

Elephant, 6½" x 8¼", (S117), $175.00-250.00; **Elephant by Palm**, 13¾" x 10¼", wedge, $275.00-350.00.

Charging Elephant, 6½" x 5⅞", $100.00-175.00; **Elephant without Tree**, 10" x 9⅞", National Foundry, (9), $175.00-250.00.

Frog on Mushroom, 4½" x 3⅝" ff-s, $175.00-225.00; **Frog**, 3½" x 6¾" ff, $100.00-175.00.

Frog, 3" x 5¼", up to $100.00; **Frog**, 2½" x 5", up to $100.00.

Frog, 6" x 3½" ff, $75.00-150.00; **Frog**, 6¾" x 4" ff, $75.00-150.00.

Frog with Black Boy, 5½" x 6½" ff, $250.00-350.00; **Advertising Frog**, 5" x 2½" ff, (I Croak for the Jackson Wagon), $125.00-200.00.

Frog, 6½" x 4½", $100.00-150.00; **Bull Frog Garden Ornament**; 9" x 4½", Hubley, $200.00-275.00.

Chameleon, 1¼" x 8", (The Sherwin Williams Paint Co.), $100.00-165.00; **Frog**, 1½" x 7½", Hubley, $125.00-200.00.

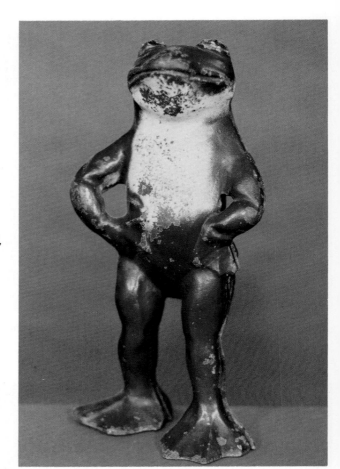

Lg. Frog, 14" x 7" ff, $1,000.00 and up.

Crocodile, 5¾" x 11½", wedge, $75.00-150.00; **Crocodile**, 2½" x 12" ff, $75.00-150.00.

Turtle, 2" x 7½", up to $100.00; **Cricket**, 2" x 9", Not to be confused with bootjack, note width of antennas, up to $100.00.

Turtle, 17" x 4¼" ff, $375.00-450.00.

Bear with Honey, 15"
x 6½" ff, $1,000.00
and up.

Lambs under Tree, 7¼" x 6⅜", $300.00-375.00; **Pinecones**, 3⅝" x 6⅞", wedge,
$125.00-200.00.

The Garden

Poppies and Cornflowers, 7¼" x 6½", Hubley, (265), $125.00-175.00; **Nasturtiums**, 7¼" x 6½", Hubley, (221), $125.00-175.00.

Delphinium, 8¾" x 7¼", Hubley, (490 Made in USA), $125.00-200.00; **Marigolds**, 7½" x 8", Hubley, (315 Made in USA), $125.00-175.00.

Jonquil, 7" x 6", Hubley, (534), $175.00-250.00; **Tulip Vase**, 10" x 8", Hubley, (443), $150.00-225.00.

Tulips, 12¾" x 6⅞", Hubley, $275.00-350.00; **Baskets of Zinnias**, 10½" x 8", $200.00-275.00.

***Narcissus**, 7¼" x 6¾", Hubley, (266), $150.00-225.00; **Modernistic Flower**, 10" x 9¾", $350.00-500.00.

Rose Basket, 11" x 8", Hubley, (121), $150.00-225.00; **Flower Basket**, 10" x 6½", $175.00-250.00.

Poppy, 10⅝" x 7⅞", Hubley, (440), $125.00-200.00; **Rose Vase**, 10⅛" x 8", Hubley, (441), $125.00-$200.00.

Petunias and Asters, 9½" x 6½", Hubley, (470), $125.00-175.00; **Gladiolus**, 10" x 8", Hubley, (489), $125.00-175.00.

Pansy Bowl, 7" x 6½", Hubley, (256), $125.00-175.00; **Violet Bowl**, 6¼" x 4¼", Hubley, (9), $125.00-175.00.

Poppies and Daisies, 7¼" x 6", Hubley, (491), $125.00-175.00; **Daisy Bowl**, 7½" x 5⅛", Hubley, (452), $100.00-150.00.

Vase of Flowers, 11¾" x 6", rk, (B&H), $250.00-325.00; **Flower Basket**, 10" x 4⅞", rk, $225.00-275.00.

Flower Bowl, 5⅞" x 5", rk, (B&H), $225.00-275.00; **Flower Basket**, 8⅝" x 5", rk, (B&H), $250.00-300.00.

Basket of Tulips, 13" x 9", Hubley, $350.00-500.00; **Rose Basket**, 12½" x 7", $250.00-300.00.

Poppy Basket, 10½" x 9½", (C H Co. E110), $325.00-450.00; **Rose Vase**, 10½" x 7" National Foundry, (145), $225.00-275.00.

Zinnias, 9¾" x 8½", Hubley, (316), $150.00-250.00; **Roses**, 8¾" x 7⅞", Hubley, (445 Made in USA), $150.00-250.00.

Flower Basket, 10" x 6", $100.00-175.00; **Flower Basket**, 9" x 6", $100.00-150.00.

Basket of Flowers, 7" x 5", Hubley, (152), $75.00-150.00; **Poppies and Snapdragons**, 7½" x 7¼", Hubley, (484), $75.00-150.00.

Apple Bossoms, 7⅝" x 5⅜", (329 Hubley), $100.00-150.00; **Flower Basket**, 8¼" x 6", (13), $100.00-150.00.

Flower Basket, 8¼" x 5¼", Hubley, others, $50.00-100.00; **Flower Basket**, 7⅞" x 5½", $75.00-150.00.

Flower Basket, 5⅞" x 5⅝", Hubley, National and Albany Foundries, $50.00-125.00; **Flower Basket**, 6½" x 5¾", (110), $75.00-125.00.

Daisy Bowl, 7" x 6", Hubley, (232), $75.00-150.00; **Zinnias**, 7¼" x 7", Hubley, (267), $125.00-175.00.

*****French Basket**, 11" x 6¾", Hubley, (69), $125.00-200.00; **Lilies of the Valley**, 10½" x 7½", Hubley, (189), $175.00-250.00.

Deco Flowers, 13¾" x 4⅝", (©△⋁△), $225.00-275.00; **Cosmos Vase**, 17¾" x 10¼", Hubley, (455), $475.00-600.00.

Flower Vase, 10⅜" x 6⅛", Hubley, (465), $175.00-250.00; **Flower Basket**, 8⅝" x 6", Hubley, (357), $150.00-225.00.

Flower Basket, 15⅞" x 7¼", National Foundry, Albany Foundry, $225.00-300.00; **Flower Basket**, 16¼" x 7⅞", (1260), cJo, $200.00-275.00.

Flower Basket, 11" x 10", Hubley, (3), $150.00-225.00; **Fruits and Flowers**, 13" x 7¼", $225.00-300.00.

Tulip Pot, 8¼" x 7", National Foundry, $175.00-250.00; **Poinsettia**, 10" x 5", (cJo 1232), $275.00-350.00.

Nasturtium, 7¼" x 6", Hubley, (301), $75.00-150.00; **Flower**, 9¼" x 6"; wedge, (⚹⚹ Pat Appl For), $175.00-250.00.

Tulips in Pot, 10½" x 5⅞", (LA-CS 770), $225.00-300.00; **Flower Pot**, 9" x 5¼", Hubley, (288), $200.00-275.00.

Flower Basket, 8⅛" x 4¾", (LA-CS 746), $175.00-250.00; **Flower Pot**, 7¼" x 5⅝", Hubley, (289), $200.00-275.00.

Flower Oval, 7⅝" x 3⅝", (B&H), $100.00-175.00; **Flower Vase**, 5¼" x 5" (cJo 1285), $100.00-175.00.

Tulips, 6⅜" x 6⅝", $75.00-150.00; **Primrose**, 7⅜" x 6¼", Hubley, (488), $125.00-200.00.

Grapes and Leaves, 7¾" x 6½", Albany Foundry, $125.00-200.00; **Goldenrods**, 7⅛" x 5½", Hubley, (268 Made in USA), $175.00-250.00.

Flower Basket, 9½" x 6½" ff, $100.00-150.00; **Flower Vase**, 7¼" x 6¼", $100.00-150.00.

Vase of Flowers, 10⅜" x 6", $200.00-275.00; **Iris**, 10⅝" x 6¾", Hubley, (469), $250.00-325.00.

Fruit Basket, 9¾" x 7½", $275.00-350.00; **Tiger Lilies**, 10½" x 6", Hubley, (472), $200.00-275.00.

Grape Bowl, 4⅛" x 7", (20), $100.00-175.00; **Fruit Bowl**, 6⅞" x 6⅝", Hubley, (456), $100.00-175.00.

Fruit Basket, 10⅛" x 7½", Albany Foundry, $175.00-250.00; **Cornucopias**, 8½" x 6", Hubley, (132), $150.00-225.00.

Flower Basket, 11" x 10⅞", $275.00-350.00; **Fruit Basket**, 11⅝" x 11⅜", $350.00-500.00.

Fruit Basket, 15⅜" x 8", Hubley, $275.00-350.00; **Fruit Basket**, 9⅝" x 6¼", $200.00-275.00.

House, Home and Miscellaneous

Cape Cod, 5¾" x 8¾", Albany Foundry, National Foundry, $125.00-200.00; **Cape Cod**, 5¾" x 8¾", (Eastern Specialty Mfg. Co.), $125.00-200.00.

Ann Hathaway's Cottage, 6⅜" x 8⅜", Hubley, $350.00-500.00; **Cape Cod Cottage**, 5½" x 7¾", Hubley, (444), $125.00-200.00.

House with Woman, 5¾" x 8½", (Eastern Spec. Mfg. Co., No 50), $300.00-500.00;
***Cottage**, 5¾" x 7½", Hubley, National Foundry, $125.00-200.00.

Fireplace, 6¼" x 8", (Eastern Specialty Co. G1), $250.00-325.00; **Cottage with Fence**, 5¾" x 8", National Foundry, (32), $125.00-200.00.

Cottage, 4⅝" x 7½", $150.00-225.00; **Cottage**, 5⅛" x 8", (AA Richardson, Quincy, Mass. Copyright), $150.00-225.00.

Cape Cod, 5" x 9¾", $175.00-250.00; **Log Cabin**, 4⅝" x 10", National Foundry, $150.00-225.00.

House, 8⅛" x 4½", (cJo 1288), $150.00-225.00; **House**, 7½" x 6⅛", (AM Greenblatt, Copyright 1927 #114), $300.00-450.00.

Sophia Smith House, 8¼" x 5½", (Birthplace of Sophia Smith), $325.00-400.00; **Two Story House**, 5⅜" x 8¾", $300.00-375.00.

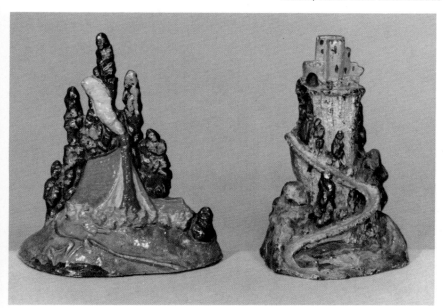

Cottage in Woods, 8¼" x 7¼", $275.00-325.00; **Castle**, 8" x 5¼", $350.00-425.00.

Cottage, 7¼" x 8½", $250.00-325.00; **Flower Basket**, 9" x 5⅜", (Creation Co. Copyr. 1930 #163), $100.00-150.00.

Flowered Doorway, 7⅝" x 7½", $325.00-405.00; **Fence**, 8" x 4¾", $150.00-225.00.

Old Mill, 6¼" x 8¼", $300.00-375.00; **Flower Basket**, 8" x 7", (#34), $100.00-150.00.

Lighthouse of Gloucester, Mass., 11½" x 9", (BA Greenblatt Studios, Boston, Mass. #8 Lighthouse of Gloucester, Mass. Copyrighted 1925), $350.00-500.00; **Lighthouse**, 14" x 7", $175.00-250.00.

Lighthouse, 7¾" x 5, (cJo 1290), $150.00-225.00; **Lighthouse**, 6¼" x 8", National Foundry, (95), $300.00-450.00.

Lighthouse, 14" x 9¼", $150.00-225.00; **Lighthouse**, 13½" x 8" ff, $150.00-225.00.

Cat, rubber, 8¾" x 4⅜", $125.00-175.00; **Lighthouse**, rubber, 9¾" x 9⅜", $250.00-300.00.

Highland Lighthouse, 9" x 7¾", (Highland Lighthouse, Cape Cod), $400.00-525.00;
Windmill, 9⅞" x 11½", (6), $450.00-600.00.

Windmill, 6¾" x 6⅞", National Foundry, (10 Cape Cod), $100.00-150.00; **Lg. Windmill**,
11⅞" x 11½", (pat pend), $350.00-425.00.

Windmill, 8" x 5⅝", (AA Richardson), $150.00-225.00; **Cape Cod**, 8¾" x 5½", (LACS), $225.00-300.00.

Outhouse, 8" x 6½", $400.00-475.00; **Ship**, 10" x 12", National Foundry, $150.00-225.00.

Clipper Ship, 11¼" x 10½", up to $100.00; **Mayflower**, 8¼" x 9", (Mayflower, Eastern Specialty Mfg. Co.), $150.00-225.00.

Ship, 9¼" x 5⅞", National Foundry, Albany Foundry, $125.00-200.00; **Fisherman at Wheel**, 6¼" x 6", $150.00-225.00.

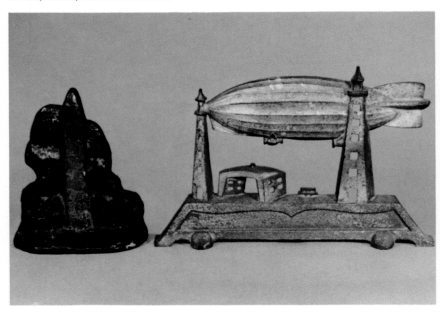

Bennington Monument, 7¾" x 6½", $175.00-250.00; **Graf Zeppelin**, 8¼" x 13", $550.00-650.00.

Pump, 8" x 6", wedge, (Cook Deep Well Pumps), $100.00-175.00; **Lighthouse**, 9½" x 6½", (Light of the World), $100.00-175.00.

Oxen and Wagon, 6¼" x 10¼", (c64), $150.00-225.00; **Conestoga Wagon**, 8" x 11", (No 100), $100.00-175.00.

London Royal Mail Coach, 7" x 12¼", (GR N17 Pat Pending, London Royal Mail Coach), up to $85.00; **Stagecoach**, 7½" x 12¼" , $75.00-125.00.

Covered Wagon, 9½" x 5⅛", Hubley, (375), $150.00-225.00; **Stagecoach**, 11¼" x 5⅞", (Hubley 376), $150.00-225.00.

Cinderella Carriage, 9¾" x 19", $150.00-225.00.

Lantern, 13" x 5", $150.00-225.00; **Harlow House**, 5" x 5", (1877 Harlow House), $125.00-200.00.

Hunter and Dog, 9½" x 8", $150.00-225.00; *__Washington Crossing Delaware__**, 8½" x 10¾", (Washington Crossing Delaware, Bicentennial 1732-1932), $175.00-250.00.

Totem Pole, 12" x 8½", $100.00-150.00; **Dolphin**, 11½" x 5½", $75.00-125.00.

Moonface, 6½" x 5", $175.00-250.00; **Cinderella Slipper**, 4" x 9", $100.00-150.00.